LoverGirl.

A.Nicole

Copyright © 2024 A. Nicole
All rights reserved.
ISBN: 979-8-9919786-1-3

Dedication

To those who never stopped believing in love and those who never stopped believing in me: This is for you!

Contents

Section One: Realizing Heartbreak Pg 1

Section Two: Love's Needs   Pg 24

Section Three: Love Yourself   Pg 32

Section Four: Love Again   Pg 39

Acknowledgements   Pg 61

Section One: Realizing Heartbreak

The Idea of You

I loved the idea of you.
The version of the fairytale I created.
I loved someone who I'm not even sure was real.
I'm living out Tamia's lyrics of Almost.
Daydreaming... night dreaming...
Selena's Dreaming of You.
I don't want to return to consciousness.
What I do want seems impossible–
Soft lips that can remove any doubts.
Kind eyes that can see to my soul.
A voice that builds me up and breaks down my walls.
An enlarged heart that has more than enough room for our future together.
I want to trace you with my almond nails
Memorizing every scar and tattoo that occupies your exterior.
I want to kiss away your internal dents caused by the outside world.
I want the reality of you,
To be like Dejavú.
I want to experience you in a way that makes me feel as though I've already loved you in a thousand lifetimes before...
Because I know that I have.

Unheard

Reminiscing on the attention,
Sometimes I get lost in the thought of you,
Then reality pops my trance.
This is not what I thought it'd be.
A beautiful friendship,
Turned into a loveless love story.
Filled with laughter, but the affection is bare minimum.
Wanted forever, but should've left in the interim.
Desires were spoken to deaf ears.
Time to wipe the tears and switch gears.

So Long

I need more compromise
This isn't working out for me.
It took you too long.
You see..

Took you too long to realize—
I was worth the commitment.
Took you too long to realize—
I was the only one in your life that was consistent.

You were so busy caring for everyone else.
Forgetting to check in with the one who you said mattered more.
Your words began to fall onto deaf ears,
And a crack formed in the foundation's core.

I sought refuge,
But ultimately ended up walking in the storm.
Letting the solitude teach me more about love
Than I've ever learned in a relationship before.

It took you too long
To notice that I was gone.

I began fleeing mentally
Before I ever left physically.

My hope is that the next one will know.
They'll see me vividly from the beginning.
I'm already aware of my worth,
So anything I attract will be enriching.

Sole Ties

Crept into my soul.
Were you even aware?
I wish you'd stop tiptoeing around the subject.
I ask what you want,
You say I deserve better.
Your response pisses me off.
I'm trying to give you a hundred and ten.
You give me the keys but won't let me within...
Within the fears, dreams, ambitions...within your love.
Somehow I always let you enter mine.
My love wraps around you tightly,
No matter how many times I let you enter & exit.
Like a pair of foamposites, form-fitting best to you.

Farewell

Letting go makes me feel like I need you,
But you actually need me.
The give and take of this relationship,
Were mainly filled with one-way streets.

I gave you every sticky drop of my love,
Until there was no more.
I shone my spotlight on you
Until others started to take notice.
I poured into you verbally
Until your cup runneth over.

You drove down Take Avenue
I took the scenic route of Giver's Street.
Every day at the congested intersection,
Is where we'd meet.

All along this journey I really thought it was me that needed you.
Yes, I needed someone to care for and place my love into,
But that person should've been me.
As soon as I realized, I knew I needed to flee.

Although I'll always love you,
I now know that you were incapable of loving me in the way I needed to receive it.

Resurrection

I'm still in love with who you used to be.
How you used to make me feel.
How your kisses felt.
How you could create a rainstorm in a drought.
I'm in love with a version of you that only few got to experience.
A version that ceases to exist.
But I bet I could make it resurface.
No matter how deep you've repressed it.
With the right amount of love.
    --A gentle love that's reserved for you only.
With the right touch.
    --A soft touch that could erase your doubts.
With the right amount of kisses all over you.
    --A kiss that has the potential to heal you in ways that only I can.
Let me resurrect the version of you that I not only fell for,
But the version that caught me.

Next Lifetime

I deleted our text thread.
Thought it would help get you out of my head.
I was wrong.
You're my unwritten, yet unforgettable song.

In my head I'm ready to risk it all, but my heart knows it isn't worth it.
Temptation can be so destructive to one's purpose.

The love has always been there, but it seems to have combusted inside of me now.
I just hope they love you like I can... but better.
You're the perfect metaphor for another lifetime.
We're like a chemical bond; I feel like our souls are embedded.

Maybe I'm making this whole thing up.
This love could be one-sided, but something tells me that you feel the connection too.
Your eyes...your smile...they tell me things
— that you will find me in our next life; I'll be your Ms. Badu.

Consistently praying for your covering.
I can only hope they'll do the same.
My heart aches
—each moment my lips speak your name.

So I remain silent.

I don't dare say aloud what I'm truly feeling.
I just pray for healing..
From the impure thoughts of you.
From the level of love I still have for you.
I pray I learn to let go so that we can both truly be happy.

Until we meet again in our next lifetimes.

Pieces

My spirit...
Broken– along with my heart. It hurts to breathe.
Inhale.
My chest is tight.
Exhale.
The pain subsides just a little.
I don't think I'm capable of loving another.
Only myself.
I'll pick up what is left of my heart and place them in the box labeled "Who I Used to Be" on the shelf.
Falling for you,
Was thought to be a dream come true.
It was the best of both worlds.
Until you decided that you weren't enough.
Couldn't come to my own conclusion.
I'm just supposed to accept yours.
The honesty got you respect
And left me broken & mangled.
I fell from my cloud of happiness.
Into a tattered photograph.
Of my past.
Shattered glass... Or was it my heart?
I knew it was fragile from the start.
Now I'm left with a piece here...and a few over there.
Can't be reassembled but maybe that's best.
Leave the pieces where they lie.
Then they can never love another guy.

Broken Scale

It makes no sense.
The scale is off.
She pushes and he pulls.
Retreating from her love.
The more he withdraws, the more her love deteriorates.
He needs to contemplate.
Is his conclusion really accurate?
Immaculate is her love.
Yet he presumes that his isn't.
Says who?
Her voice is overpowered by his.
He sees her as inadequate of making her own ethical decision.
But he can't see that he's diminishing her spirit.
Her heart is shattered.
Lost the only thing that really mattered…
The ability to love.

Broken, but Okay

You enter the room.
You see her sitting there.
An empty box on her lap labeled *MEMORIES*.
You ask why it's empty.
She tells you it's full.
You explain it's nothing there.
She proceeds to explain it to you:

*"In here are my memories.
Broken hearts and smiles.
Tears and laughter.
These memories last for miles.
I once was a broken soul.
Then I realized all these things make me whole.
They made me.
I thought they would break me...
But in tragedy, comes triumph.
I had to refuse to give up."*

You're looking at the tears staining her face.
Longing for a smile to take their place.
She whispers—

*"Don't pity me.
If anything, you should envy me.
I'm human, I will break down.
Sometimes it happens when there are a million people around.
But I never feel ashamed
Because everyone has experienced pain.
They've sat where I'm sitting now."*

No words escape you.
You accept all hers as being true.
Because you have to.
You are one.
She's looking into the eyes of her future.
You're looking into the eyes of the present-day.

Both acknowledging silently, that you're broken right now but you'll be okay.

Fraudulent

Say you don't care.
Say there's nothing there.
But I'm aware…
I'm not the one in need.
So I'll leave.
It'll be hard as hell, but I'll get through it.
Everything—
You're going to miss it.
You pushed me to my limit.
Said I could do better, you've gotten your wish.
I'm gone.
But it's okay
Because one day,
You'll wish you never parted your lips.
Wish you would've taken full advantage of this.

Although–
I have turned back in the past,
And I can't guarantee that the last time was my last.
I can guarantee moving on is what I'll try.
Just wanted you to be that guy.
I blame myself.
I sold myself the dream.
But you were a good realtor as well.
Let me think everything was what it seemed.

Hate To Love You

I hate you.
For making me feel beautiful.
For making me feel special.
For making me feel as though you had fallen face first into something amazing with me.
For making me feel like I was the only one you wanted...
I would've respected raw honesty.
But most of all I hate you for being you.
Because I fell in love.

Silly Me

All I ever wanted was your love.
For you to look into a room full of people and only see me.
To express your feelings as easily as I can express mine.
Searching for reciprocity.
From you to me.
Should be done easily.
So why do I feel like I'm pulling teeth.
Stop looking at the forest and focus on the tree in front of you.
I wish you'd understand that my heart is starting to give way.
Though I can't really say you're all to blame.
I knew the situation but proceeded anyway.
Silly me…
The hopeless romantic
Who's fallen in love with her best friend.
But he can't let his truths come from within.
So she waits…
Her patience is just temperamental.
Hot and cold.
She'd give him the world.
Her world.
She just wants his embrace.
Too much to ask I guess.
Who knows how long this charade will last.
Silly me…
I'm trapped again.
One foot out and one foot in.
Just waiting…
Waiting for you to ask me to stay.

Love To Be Loved

I see you.
I feel your energy.
I know you would love to be loved.

To have someone acknowledge your power and your pain.
To bring a balance to your tilted world.
To reassure you daily of your significance in their life.

You crave someone that prioritizes you.
You crave the security of knowing you can be at peace.
You crave the ability to be as soft as melted butter.

I know you would love to be loved..
Because I would love to be loved too.

Truthfully, there is someone who would love to love you.
Hold you tight and lay next to you each night.

There is someone who would love to love me as well...
They're out there somewhere.
Their soul wandering, looking for mine.
Aimlessly passing the time.
Waiting for their complimentary life partner.

They would love to be loved.
Cared for.
Heard.
Understood.

You're lucky if you receive the love that you're longing for.
Because we're all just longing to be loved in the way that we desire.

To All The Weak Hearts

Loving isn't for your kind.
It's watery eyes & smiles.
Lonely nights & amazing climaxes.
All mixed together.
Never knowing which way is up.
What's the measurement of your cup?
Half empty or half full?
Just half.
In between.
Straddling the fence.
Your heart's convinced..
Brainwashed.
But your brain wants no parts.
It swears it knows better.
Or is it confused with bitter?
Insecurities hidden behind a disguise.
Those big, beautiful cinnamon eyes,
That look upon the world with admiration & determination
To change this crazy place.
Let the heart win the race
At a reasonable pace.
It just needs to be worked out,
Like any other muscle; a part of the beautiful physique of the human frame.
Ask the dearly departed,
Loving isn't for the weak-hearted.

Section Two: Love's Needs

Tell Her She's Beautiful.

Remind her
Of how you admire—
Lips the softest baby pink.
Skin that's been kissed by caramel itself.
Eyes that hold the sun captive.
A crown made up of the finest coils
      —soft and black with a red tint only noticed by you when she sunbathes.
Freckles and moles that are the constellations of her body.
Pierced twin peaks
      —one covering a heart filled with the purest form of love.
Tattoos that tell a story of how she loves her family and learned to love herself.
Stretch-marks that cover the ass and thighs that you love to use to keep you warm.
The daintiest hands that can bring you pleasure or comfort
      —depending on what you need.
A speaking voice that she hates
      —but you love it just as much as her singing voice.
Beauty is encapsulated in her...
Wrapped inside her God-chosen DNA.
So why haven't you told her?
Why haven't you reminded her?
She's well aware of her beauty,
But she needs to hear it from you.
To feel seen.
To feel appreciated.
To feel loved.
So tell her she's beautiful...
And watch how your favorite smile illuminates the room.

Trophy Wife

Wading through life's ocean
Becoming a bit tarnished
Trying not to drown
There have been so many moments…
Moments when she was close to the edge.
Overstimulated.
Overspent.
But there's always been a sparkle in her.
Even when it dimmed down,
Those who loved her could always see it.
Pouring into her cup when she's depleted.
They see her beauty even on her ugliest days.
Reminding her that she's a trophy nonetheless.
Regardless of how she feels or how she sees herself in the moment—
She's a trophy.
The prize in the arcade that you spent endless hours collecting tickets to get.
She's Aladdin's lamp *and* the genie inside.
She's a phenomenal woman who will make a phenomenal wife.
She's held together by prayers, tears, and love.
Built up by hugs, laughter, and sunshine.
Although she knows all the above,
Some days she can't fathom it…
Can't see her own greatness.
Can't see the beauty in her smile
Or the warmth in her honey eyes.
But she's always reminded—
Even though she's not the trophy wife she'd envisioned that she'd be,
She's still a trophy, nonetheless.

Loudly

Handholding.
Kisses.
Opening doors.
Give me all that plus more.
Wrap your arms around my waist in a room full of people...
In a way that makes time stop and makes me only see you.
Never forget the sidewalk rule.
Take me and sway to the beat that only we can hear.
Sit across from me during meals,
Because you love the way my face lights up when I'm speaking passionately.
Surprise me with "just because" flowers,
Even though you know I buy my own.
Turn your phone on Do Not Disturb,
Just because you want to watch a movie together.
Forehead kisses on any occasion.
Hugs to decompress bad days.
Sensual groping in public and private.
Laugh uncontrollably with me because I'm silly when I'm tired.

Love me passionately.
Love me kindly.
Love me proudly.
Love me strongly.
Love me fearlessly.
Love me **loudly**.

Unrealistic

Am I wrong for wanting the fairytale?
Glass slippers & wicked witches I can do without.
Just undying love,
From a God-made spouse.
Am I wrong for wanting forehead kisses and handheld walks?
Is it too much to ask for cuddling & pillow talk?
Our bodies tangled together every night.
Sensual kisses,
Forceful grabs & caresses.
Occasional scratches & bites.
The fairytale doesn't exist in present-day society.
But I can easily create a personal fairytale for you and me.
Unrealistic expectations
In a realistic world.
But I can definitely try to make them **MY** reality.
  –Forever, the hopeless romantic girl.

Don't Just Tell Her She's Beautiful

Tell her she's intoxicating instead.
Tell her that you replay your last exchange with her in your head.
Tell her that you admire her heart.
Tell her that she's a work of art.
Tell her that she leaves you breathless, but in a good way.
Tell her she's the best part of every especially long day.
Tell her that her resilience is one of the main things that draws you in.
Tell her how she's your best friend.

Don't just tell her she's beautiful...
Although it's nice to hear.
Vocalize how she leaves your heart full...
How her voice is the sweetest melody that travels through your ears.

Tell her that you adore her strength, but with you she can be fragile.
Tell her that her problems are not just hers, but also yours to handle.
Tell her that you love watching her sleep.
Tell her how you love it because you know that she's at peace.
Tell her that you value her opinion.
Tell her that it's because you know she thinks everything though with precision.
Tell her that the way she walks makes you hypnotized.
Tell her that she is the only one who makes you want to compromise.

Don't just tell her she's beautiful...
She's pretty self-aware.
Articulate how you love that she makes you feel fully capable...
And that's there's nothing or no one who can compare.

Tell her that she forces you to think and grow.
Tell her that with her is where your heart feels at home.
Tell her that laying your head on her chest is your bad day's antiserum.
Tell her that she's the reason for your optimism.
Tell her that her laughter can shift the trajectory of your day.
Tell her that you miss her presence whenever she's away.
Tell her that there's nothing you enjoy more than making her smile.
Tell her that she's the reason you will forever go the extra mile.

Don't just tell her she's beautiful.
Tell her that her soul captivates yours.
Show her that her love makes mountains moveable.
Show her that your love is one that reassures.

Want (Loudly Part 2)

I want love...
A deeply profound, reciprocated love.
A love that brings me flowers because it's Thursday.
A love that makes my blood boil & my heart flutter all at once.
I want that "I want a love like that couple" love.
I want that "scream it to the mountaintops" love.
I want that "you're the only one I love" love.
I want that love that isn't afraid to be seen or put on display.
I want that love that every girl longs to have but very few do because they never experienced self-love.
I want that fairytale love that young girls often grow up believing in.
I want the love that loves me for me.
I want that movie love.
The butterflies every time we kiss love.
The touch that sends electricity through my entire body and torches my soul love.
I want that love that isn't just mine.
I want that love that's ours.
I want more than a love that is me and you, I want a love that is me *PLUS* you.
I want a love that gives.
I want that love that makes me cry occasionally because it is so beautiful.
I want a love that inspires.
I want that love that seems magical even during the darkest of times.
Most of all, I want a love that inspires me to be a better person.

Section Three: Love Yourself

Until They Do

This is for the girl who's lost her spark.
The one who's loved and been left broken.
The one who's wandering.
The one who's feeling like she's not where she should be.
The girl who's poured into everyone else, but never had someone quench her soul's thirst.

Someone will come along...

Someone who will water you and watch you bloom.
Someone who will jumpstart your heart.
Someone who will wipe your tears and make you laugh all in the same breath.
Someone who will reassure your place in life.
Someone who will wrap you up in a hug that will melt away any day's stressors.

But until they do...

Water your soul's garden.
Buy yourself the flowers.
Learn to dance in the storms.

Take yourself on dates.
Look good for *YOU*.
Let your energy transform.

The day will come when you're no longer left wandering or wondering, but your heart will be in a constant state of fluttering.

Solar Powered

She recharges from the sun.
Barefoot and happy.
Drawn to the warmth of the sea.
Her smile is as warm as a summer breeze.
It's a magnificent, magnetic force.
Like the sun, she draws you in.
Her spirit energizes,
Hopping right into your heart,
Electrifying your life,
Bringing a vibrancy unlike anything else...
Unmatched.
She's the center of your solar system.
The brightest star you see:
So bright that you can still see her in your sleep.
She's the solar panels over the roof of your life—
Powering your love.
Restoring your faith in God nightly.
Regenerating your damaged cells.
There's no need to plug in,
Because you're spiritually connected.
She is merely a socket...
A portal for you to experience a glimpse of God's love.

Available

A pure, finite love.
A love that soothes your soul.
A love that calms your crazy.
A love that abolishes your anxiety.

A love that quenches.
A love that does.
A love that warms.
A love that carries.

An agape love.
A love that is child-like.
A love that is not judgmental.
A love that is empathetic.

A love that teaches.
A love that grows.
A love that prays.
A love that restores.

I'm only available for genuine love.

Dear Love

You're a walking love letter–

Filled with endless metaphors and similes.
Written in the prettiest black calligraphy.
Complimenting whoever is the reader.
Smelling like their favorite memory.
You were sealed with passion.
Delivered as a high-priority package.

Alternate Ariel

Lost in the sea of our love.
Swept away by the riptide.
Thought I would be the reverse Little Mermaid…
I didn't want legs;
Just wanted to swim in your habitat.
Instead I drowned.
Lost consciousness and ultimately myself.
But I was reborn in the water.
A renewed version is emerging.
Just.
Keep.
Swimming.
I'm almost back at shore.
Back at peace.
Back in love…
But this time, with me.

The Ask

Deserving of the deepest desires your spirit craves.
Worthy of having a partner who won't solidify your heart.
An addition for you in every aspect,
Because you're whole on your own.
Anything they provide is gratuity.
You'd be surprised what you could have wholeheartedly,
If you simply ask and stop settling.

Section Four: Love Again

Extinguish

What started as a lit candle quickly became a 5-alarm fire
—because I'm a pyro.
Like a moth to a light,
I keep coming back even though I know it's my downfall.
The warmth draws me in but it's ultimately going to kill me.

I'm going to die either way.
So, I might as well speak my last words into the flame
And watch them fall into the ashes.

Truth is, I love you.
Always have.
Always will.
There's nothing that can take away that. Creatively, I feel safe with you.
Your conversation is a constant cliff-hanger;
 —I always need more.
I envision your charming smile and deep brown eyes.
 —smile smoother than silk
 —eyes capable of reading me better than a polygraph.
Your hugs bring a warmth that ignites me internally.
I can't dare speak your name.
But I want you to have your flowers while you're still around to enjoy them.

Maybe this is all just in my head.
The fire…
The feeling…
The flashbacks…

Maybe I should just suppress all this,
Take the chance of letting it build up and cause spontaneous combustion.

Worth the Weight

I've been carrying around this burden
This burning love for you.
No matter how many times I try to extinguish it—
It just reignites.

Varying from a slow burn to a blaze.
A three-alarm fire rings through your gaze.

No one has even awoken my spirit like you.
Simple conversation.
A loving hug.
A playful joke.
Oh— and my favorite, the forehead kiss.
All are like gasoline for my soul.

I waited for my chance to catch the train to your heart...
I boarded but I didn't have enough fare for the whole trip.
Now I'm carrying around my luggage...
Looking for a good place to sit it.

Although the journey was short-lived.
I regret nothing.
Loved and lost is what I did.
But I walked away with something.

I left with a fire of memories to keep my heart warm.
I left knowing that my heart will always sing this song.
I left knowing that the weight I'll carry around forever is worth it.
I left knowing that I was once loved in the way that I deserved it.

The wait that I endured to get to your heart back then, is well worth the weight that I'll continue to carry.

Back Here

We always end up back here.
Me craving your touch
And wondering if you're craving mine.
Each lying in the dark in what feels like opposite ends of the earth…
Sending seismic waves
Hoping that they can reach.
Phone's on silent.
But steadily checking it.
Making sure there's no missed notifications.
Too stubborn to admit our faults.
Waiting for one another to crack…
Crack a joke,
Crack a smile,
Just crack anything other than our hearts.
            —They've been through enough.
Radio silence throughout the night.
An eerie calm.
The sun awakes both your souls.
Three dots.
On both ends.
Here it comes…
We're back.

More…

Than my favorite constellation,
Than the perfect sunny day at the beach,
Than all my dreams that are within reach.

Than the perfect sunset,
Than the most beautiful bouquet,
Than enjoying a snow day.

Than a sunflower adoring the sun,
Than any prized possession,
Than any obsession.

I love you more than all the things that life may bring.
I love you more than my favorite lyrics to sing.

I love you more than any wealth I can obtain.
I love you more than I'll ever love again.

Your Love

I equate your love to a forehead kiss from my favorite.
It warms my soul.
Makes me feel as though everything is right in the world.
 I can move mountains with my mustard seed of faith..
All because of your love.

It fuels my spirit.
Makes me feel as though I can achieve my wildest dreams.
All my goals are attainable.
I'm fueled by the magic of your hugs.
All because of your love.

Attraction

What was once simplistic beauty that I wouldn't second glance at,
Has become enchanting.
Sucking me in like a black hole,
Despite my resistance.
Like Protons and neutrons we can't resist each other.
Complimenting one another and forming something greater.
Two making up one.
Coming undone,
We're just ordinary.
Extraordinary in our most delicate form as a whole.
Crazy how I can't leave you alone.
Like the opposite ends of a magnet, we attract.
Always lingering and willing to distract;
With a sweet smile…
A hearty, shared laugh…
No matter how many times we separate,
We continue to cross paths.

Rooted

You showed me yours.
I showed you mine.
Our hearts were on full display for one another.
Never questioning the love that grew,
Between me and you.
You were my multicolored sunshine.
I was your evening star;
Guiding each other through.
We were an amplitude unmatched and unheard of.
The slightest amount of eye contact.
Tracing me with just a fingertip.
The way you said my name.
It all drove me insane... in a good way.

Did you know that your touch could solar power my soul?
Did you know that your confirmation still helps me grow?
A million gratitude's could never be enough
To give my appreciation for all you've done.

My head is often in the clouds,
Romanticizing a fairy tale that I may never get to read.
Despite my rose-colored outlook,
You always gave me the confidence to believe...
Believe that I was...
Deserving.
Beautiful.
Creative.
You nurtured me in the same way I've always nurtured everyone else.

Never had I ever felt a love that was so God-like and inspiring.
Recharging my spirit and mending broken pieces.
Caring for me in a way I didn't expect.
In a way that I could never regret.
You gave me your whole heart
And I gave you mine.
I hope you know you'll carry mine with you
Throughout the rest of our many lifetimes
You're rooted in my mind, heart, and soul.
So deep that it will always continue to blossom for seasons to come.

A Love Letter

As I lay beside you quietly,
Listening to your heartbeat.
Studying the patterns of your breaths.
I feel that you were made for me.
No other arms have felt safer.
No kiss as sweet.
No touch as caring.

No embrace as comforting.
No smile as warm as yours.
It's amazing how much better I sleep at night when you're beside me.
I used to wonder if soulmates were a real thing.
They are.
You're mine.

As I can hear you breathing
I wonder what you're dreaming.
I'll lay closer to you in case the dream is not so pleasant.
So you'll awake and know I'll always be here.
By your side.
Ready to console you.
Ready to uplift you.
Ready to build with you.

Ready to love you unconditionally, above all. I lay awake and think of how we got here.
All the years put in that never seemed to work because the timing was wrong. All the random texts with lyrics from your favorite songs.
The arguments that led to silence for months on end. The unfeigned laughs that captured where it all began.

When you awake in the morning and find this letter,
I can only hope it'll make your day that much better.
Your offset smile and plump peach lips have a way of warming my soul.
I look back at where we started years ago and I'm excited to see how this story unfolds.
I look forward to every single day with you.
Even on the nights when your snoring keeps me up, like now.

This love is my favorite song on repeat with the volume up loud.

As the moon gets relief from the sun,
I lay here and pray that we'll always be one.
I pray I'll write out my love to you until we both become stars in the sky.
I pray you'll never doubt I love you but instead know all the reasons why.

Jesse's Son

You're a version of King David reincarnated.
You've always known you were destined—
For something superior.
For unwavering love.
Worthy of all the praise—
Even when it was rarely given.
Trials and tribulations help shape you.
Though unkind, one might say they were necessary.
Without them, you wouldn't have blossomed in the dark.
A spark recharging all those who you let get close.
A soul who didn't let the world completely crystalize his heart.
Like David when he defeated Goliath,
You've always known that God planted something great inside of you.
You've always been equipped with the proper tools.
People counted you out but you ran your own race.
Against all odds.
Once you moved forward,
You took off.
The levels you've reached thus far,
It's unexplainable, but not unbelievable.
It's God.
It's your trust in Him.
It's your faith in knowing that everything you want, God wants for you too.
Jesse's youngest son always had more faith than that of a mustard seed.
Which is why God gave him so much.
Your faith has always seemed so unfaltering.
Which is why God is treating you as such.
Just as David went astray—
He knows you won't be perfect either.
But He instilled in you that spark..
So use it to light your path in this season.

Like to Love

Like the necessity of summer rain,
Like the inside of a geode always sparkles,
Like every inch of my skin craves shea butter,
Like Christians need the gospel,

Like the planets need to orbit around the sun,
Like we need to breathe clean air,
Like growing up can't be avoided,
Like conditioner is essential for coily hair,

Like we need to have faith,
Like we all need water to grow,
Like everything needs to be recharged,
Like the stars will always glow,

You'll always have a piece of my heart and a portion of my love.

Platonic

Soulmates that were never meant to be,
You and me.
We fell so incredibly deep.
The price we paid was not cheap.

Sacrificed our love for friendship.
Our hearts we had to re-equip.
But they still have a grip.

Although our love had to shift.
I'll always be thankful for this gift.
True, unbiased, unfiltered, honest, gentle: love.

Always You

I've been fantasizing of our future.
An alternate reality from the one we currently reside in.
In the future I envision, we're together:
The family we always talked about.
Laughing, building, and praying together.
A family built on God's love.
Pouring from our faith overflow,
Into the foundations of our children.
Displaying a true love of God and one another.
Accessorizing each other in only a way that we can…
No substitutes can love you better than I and vice versa.
It was always you.
In my heart and in my mind.
Propelling me into my greatness.
Allowing me to be soft.
It was always you.

Summertime Sunshine

A kiss from your lips is like a gust of wind at the shore in 95-degree weather.
The perfect relief.
Blowing through my imperfect twists and landing right on the nape of my neck.
Nothing will ever taste sweeter to me.

You fill my soul with an indescribable belief—
Belief in myself.
Belief in you.
Belief in our future.
Helping me to see every glass as half full,
Yet still topping me off.
Always anticipating my needs and learning to still cater to my wants.
Asking for confirmation instead of assuming.

You've become a consistent contributor–
To my happiness.
To my growth.
To my mental health.

You're the perfect beach day–
Refueling me with your warm love and waves of affection.
All while being 70SPF and covering me from harm.
I enjoy watching you shine.

Fairytales

In need of romance sprinkled with lust.
A weak-knees, organ-pulsing whirlwind.
Something that can spike my temperature.
Beyoncé can be crazy in love;
I want to be calm in love... understood in it.
Take my breath away, but don't cut off my air supply.
Whisk me away, but don't violently uproot me.
Let me live in a fairytale, but don't build it with lies.
Speak your truth to me, gently.
I'll center you in peace.

Regret

I wish I would've never pushed away your kiss.
It still lingers on my lips and in my mind.
Your embrace is something I long for each day.
The perfect beginning, middle, and end to each one.
Right one, wrong timing.
Right place, now I'm left longing.
The warmth between our embraces,
Could warm the Arctic Tundra.
Truthfully, I don't know what unsettles me more...
The fire we create or the regret I have for pouring water over the flame.
The moment replays on a loop--
You pull me in,
Hands strong and cozy
Our kiss remains for eternity.
As does the guilt for bruising your heart—
Embedded in my soul.

Bilingual

I want to be fluent in you.
Speaking affirmations that only you understand.
Showing you how much I love not only who you are now,
But who you will eventually become.
Spending time practicing my dictation with you,
Until I properly sound out every vowel.
You aren't my native language,
But you've easily become my favorite.

My Black Man

Bronze skin that is almost golden.
Shimmering even in the dark of night.
Ringlets soft and bushy as wool.
Perfectly plump lips with a physique to match…
Every detail about him is the cherry on top.
His heart speaks a language that only mine is fluent in.
No matter the distance, we'll always find our way back to one another.
His arms—
      help to carry my load…
      lift my spirits…
      and hold me together.
His smile—
      warms the coldest day…
      brings calmness…
      makes my lips reciprocate.
His voice—
      stills my anxiety…
      provides reassurance that I'm not alone…
      and declares his love for me.
A man of many talents,
But my favorite is his magic.
Melanin magic filling me to the brim
      —with endless possibilities of faith and growth.
      —with endless possibilities of life and laughter.
Overflowing my life with the reality of a fairytale I dreamt for myself as a young Tiana.
I've been enlisted to be loved by a black man.
One of the rarest forms of love there is.
Commissioned to build a place of peace.

Our Galaxy

You're the Perseids
And I'm the onyx sky.
You illuminate me.
When I speak of you, the roses in my cheeks are in full bloom
And the sun shines through my pupils.
Even on my darkest nights,
I find peace in knowing you're orbiting my heart.
Passionately holding on to the memories we created,
And longing to create a new galaxy where only we exist.
But for now, you're just the meteors that pass through my soul…
Keeping my hope for love lit.

The Effect

Each kiss more sensual than the last.
Traces of honey linger for days.
Just a glimpse of you and my heart jumps.
I turn into putty and you scoop me up;
Using my love languages to mold me.
Building me back into the goddess I forgot that I was.
The energy between us is enough to light the abyss.
Felt in our touch…
In our kiss…
In our text messages.
A safe love that grows exponentially.
That's what you've always been to me.
All our sides have been shown,
But we never run.
Growing into something we never thought we'd be.

Thanks

For loving me
All of me.
For seeing my heart.
For pouring into my soul. For handling me with care.
For supplying the love you know that I so desperately needed.
For believing in my dream
Even when I had forgotten it.
For helping to restore my faith.
For being patient while I healed.
For reminding me of my greatness.
Thank you.

Acknowledgments

Although I titled it LoverGirl.; I wrote this for the lover inside all of us. No matter what phase of love you currently reside in, my hope is that you will see yourself or someone you love in this collection.

Mom and Dad, you both have always made me feel loved. Once you found out I enjoyed writing, you planted the seed that I would be a published author. Now the mustard seed has sprouted. Thank you for always reminding me that nothing is out of my reach.

Thank you to Bean (Eliza), Brittany, Eric, and Mia for being my test readers. Brittany, thank you so much for being my accountability partner throughout writing this and for pushing me to keep going even when I was doubting myself. You poured into me more than you even realized. Bean, thank you for reminding me of my greatness, always.

To my lovely ladies who constantly pour into me; Tynesha, Tyeisha, Bria, Wynesa, Whitney, Kendra, Lyndsie and Farrah, thank you!!! Having you alongside me on my journey has made more of an impact than you know. Whitney, your friendship for the past 25 years is a true testament of platonic love. No matter the physical distance between us, you have ALWAYS supported me and my dreams. Ty, Tye, and Nesa, the love you three have given me over the past 16 years has healed me in ways that I never thought friendship could. Thank you for always holding space for me, especially when it comes to matters of the heart. Bria and Farrah, you both are prime examples that people can come into your life and want more for you/support you more than someone who has been in your life for years. Kendra and Lyndsie, you both have always been cheering me on whether near or far and always remind me of who and whose I am. I will always be honored that God sent you all to me.

To my big sissy Maia, I love you. You inspired me all those years ago to be a better poet and to never shy away from sharing my gift with others. You have helped me find my strength time and time again. I will forever be thankful for your encouragement and unconditional love.

To everyone who has read my poetry over the years and gave me the extra push to finally write this book, THANK YOU! Your encouragement truly means the world to me.

Finally, to those that I have loved and still love, thank you for being my muses. Without you, this book would not be possible.

www.ingramcontent.com/pod-product-compliance
Lightning Source LLC
Chambersburg PA
CBHW070858050426
42453CB00012B/2256